ENVISIONING VIRTUAL REALITY

ENVISIONING VIRTUAL REALITY

A TOOLKIT FOR IMPLEMENTING VR IN EDUCATION

MEREDITH THOMPSON, DAVID KASER, AND KARA GRIJVALA

Carnegie Mellon University: ETC Press

Pittsburgh, PA

Contents

Part I. Overview

1.   Introduction   3

2.   Making Virtual Reality a Reality in Today's   5
Classrooms
Meredith Thompson

3.   Imagining VR for Education in the Developing   17
World

Part II. The "How To's" of VR Integration

4.   Three Levels of VR Integration   41
David Kaser and Meredith Thompson

5.   VR in K12   49
Building a Program from the Ground Up
David Kaser and Meredith Thompson

6.   Student Voice Counts   60
Assessing VR Applications
David Kaser and Meredith Thompson

7. Viewing Virtual Reality from the Students'   72
    Perspective
    David Kaser and his students

8. Conclusion   86

    Part III. About the Authors

9. Meredith Thompson Ed.D.   91

10. David Kaser   94
    STEM Teacher - Barberton High School

11. Kara Grijalva   97

    Part IV. Appendix

12. The Raven VR Sample Lesson   101
    David Kaser and his students

13. VR App Evaluation   108
    David Kaser

    About the ETC Press   113

Part I

Overview

I

INTRODUCTION

———————

Even as the virtual ink is drying on this collection of articles, the technological landscape for VR is evolving. We have seen in the last two months of summer 2019 the introduction of standalone headsets with 6 Degrees of Freedom (6 DoF) and the elimination of external tracking sensors in commercial VR technology. In the last two years, we have seen the price point drop to reach a mainstream audience. No doubt, these advances will continue and what once had a "wow" factor will be commonplace.

These chapters contain specific examples highlighting various classroom models that utilize virtual reality with the goal of making this innovation feasible and sustainable in a wide range of settings. We take time to discuss easily overlooked setup details that are vital to successful implementation, share ideas about how to curate classroom content, work with teachers, and maintain the technology once it's purchased. We also provide the unique perspective of high school students, who share their own experiences with VR. All of this is done to illustrate how VR might be used from low resource environments to classrooms blessed with a strong financial backing.

Even though the topic is virtual reality, the examples and teaching practices contained in these pages have ideas about feasibility and sustainability that carry lasting relevance in the face of ever-changing technology. We hope you will join us in considering how to expand students' experiences and interaction with content through these new technologies, and encourage you to share them with us at envisionXR.net.

MAKING VIRTUAL REALITY A REALITY IN TODAY'S CLASSROOMS

Meredith Thompson

The market for virtual reality applications is growing at a rapid pace, and is expected to double in the next 5 years (Bolkan, 2017). As the cost of equipment falls and schools have greater access to technology, there is great interest in virtual reality as an educational tool. A small but growing group of educators have started to integrate virtual reality in their classrooms with promising results (Castaneda, Cechony & Bautista, 2017; Zimmerman, 2019). We reached out to teachers and administrators who are currently using virtual reality in their classrooms to hear their perspectives and practical strategies for infusing this resource into their classrooms. Teachers have creative ideas for how to incorporate immersive education in current classrooms: how to select activities, how to set up the classroom, how to get support during the activity, and how to transport devices. Teachers also shared their ideas for future applications of VR, including how to deepen the learning experience and to expand the reach of these technologies to a greater population of students. Here we share three vignettes of three different approaches: a social studies class in a suburban school district, a district-wide perspective from an urban school district, and a class designed entirely around understanding and implementing VR for other classrooms. We also share how we are using these ideas to inform our own project in designing a collaborative immersive virtual reality educational game for introductory high school biology.

Students from Gloucester Biotech Academy try Cellverse, a VR game about cellular biology

Exploring the World from Within the Classroom Walls

Part of learning about immigration in Melinda Lohan's high school classroom in Medfield, MA is a virtual visit to both Ellis

Island and Angel Island. "Most of my students have been to Ellis Island but most haven't been to Angel Island", Lohan explains, "They can see two entry points for immigration and how it has changed based on the current political climate". Lohan has been using virtual field trips in her class for three years, after being introduced to the experiences during a digital learning day sponsored by the technology specialists in Medfield. Students use their own phones during the activity, and the school supplies the viewers. Initially, there was some turbulence. "The first time I tried it, it was totally a disaster. The Wi-Fi didn't work; the students could not get set up". Now she asks her students to download the field trip app to their phones on the first day of school as a homework assignment, and asks the students to keep the application on their phone or accessible in the cloud for easy access. "The more you can set up in advance, the easier it will be".

Using a flipped classroom model, Lohan's students watch her lectures on YouTube and do their notes at home, which gives them time to focus on activities during class. She provides guiding questions to keep them focused on the learning objective, but lets students choose how they watch the virtual reality field trips. "There is a lot of movement in the field trips and so they can get dizzy. I let them do what they want – stand, sit, lie down on the floor. I also have a screen so they can mirror a phone for the group in case the Wi-Fi cuts out." Lohan's experience with virtual field trips is evident when she quickly adds, "I make sure to tell the students to turn off their notifications before they share their screen with anyone. Once I did not tell the kids to turn off their notifications, and a snapchat came up while we were looking at one student's phone. She was mortified. So, now I always remind them at the start of class." The school helpdesk, staffed by high school students, also provides support if the Wi-Fi is variable or the devices are not working properly.

Lohan has found many ways to weave the field trips to her curriculum. Students virtually visit the Tenement Museum when they talk about Industrialization, and visit the Normandy Beaches and the Holocaust Museum when they do their unit on World War II. The field trips turn social studies into an active learning experience, and her students are eager to try them out. Lohan is also strategic about how often she uses virtual field trips in her unit plans. "The kids love them, however, I think whenever you do something too frequently the students get immune to it. We don't go on a field trip every chapter. If you do it every single time then it's not as engaging".

Thinking ahead, Lohan would love to have students be able to make and test critical decisions in history. "I'd like them to be able to make decisions that could change history. To decide on whether or not you're going to have the draft of what you're factories are going to look like. I wish they had access not only to view but also to create. That's when they learn the most – not by looking at someone else's work, but by creating their own".

Coordinating Cross-District Logistics

For the past 2 years, Chris Turner and Paula Giaquinto have helped teachers integrate virtual reality into their classrooms in Fitchburg, MA. The experience of integrating virtual reality lessons in 8 different schools ranging from elementary to high school has made them masters of logistics. "We have a pack of 30 phones and smaller packs of 5 phones that are district resources." Giaquinto explains. "We have kits and containers that Chris has designed, and they are pretty mobile." One challenge they have faced sharing the equipment across multiple classes is keeping the devices charged. To address this issue, Turner repurposed photography carrying cases into portable "tech tubs" complete with rapid charging cords so the devices can be charged easily and compactly in between classes. Giaquinto adds, "We schedule times to charge the devices".

Before class, they set up the devices on a counter or table, and get the screens lit up and on the school's Wi-Fi network. Once the teacher's laptop is activated, they distribute the devices table by table. Different age ranges pose different challenges. In the middle and high school, teachers see multiple classes, so they can set up the equipment in one classroom. In the elementary school, the virtual reality equipment moves from class to class since classes are self-contained. Once the devices are transported, the distributing 30 devices to eager elementary students can be a challenge, so volunteer parents also help the teachers in class. Turner and Giaquinto have also created smaller sets of devices. Giaquinto explains, "We've had most success with the smaller groups. We have about 5-6 students interacting with the VR where others are rotating through centers or other activities they are involved with".

"Our district demographics are challenging", Giaquinto explains, "we are an urban district in north central Massachusetts. Even though we are less than an hour from the ocean, many students have never been to the beach." These virtual field trips have brought Fitchburg students to the desert, the rainforest, and to the tundra to experience the Northern Lights. Chris recounts a story about a class who was viewing the YouTube movie "Elephants on the Brink" after reading parts of the novel *A Long Walk to Water*. "One child was so engrossed in the video experience that when someone went by and brushed their shoulder – the child exclaimed 'the elephant touched me!' – these experiences are absolutely immersive."

Finding available applications is a joint effort between the administration and the teachers. Thus far, teachers have primarily drawn from Google Expeditions, Discovery Learning, and YouTube education. The STEM coordinator in the district, Jessica Stodulski has collected a number of resources, as well as the content coaches for math and English as a second language. The teachers in the district are contributing too. When resources are unavailable, the teachers are creating their own. They recorded a field trip to the butterfly garden to bring to the elementary school students during their unit on monarch migration. After talking with a competitor in the Iditarod dogsled race, they asked them to film the experience. Giaquinto explains, "I believe last year the group that was involved in the race was filming VR footage for us for this year -t hat's still in progress."

Now that teachers are experienced in using virtual reality in their classroom, the Fitchburg technology team plans to incorporate more interactive virtual reality equipment that allows students to interact with each other. They are currently investigating Oculus Rifts and Vive. "Right now, the field trips are mostly guided – we would like to have students fully participating in this. Right now the way we have used virtual reality is strategic but it's parallel play. We want to have students take information and try things and test things out in the virtual world".

Creating an Educational Virtual Reality Lab

The students come into David Kaser's classroom and gather their tools from two different carts – a laptop and a backpack containing an Oculus Rift. It takes about 10 minutes for the class of 19 students will set up 10 Oculus Rifts around the classroom. "It looks pretty spectacular, but it's chaotic", David comments, "since we use the classroom for other things, so that doesn't allow me to leave the VR set up permanently." The students are currently selecting and analyzing applications that use immersive 3D virtual reality within the classroom, however, the experience Kaser's high school students gain in setting up and breaking down the Oculus Rifts and laptops will soon come in handy. After the students curate a database of VR activities, the class will transition from evaluating educational applications to supporting teachers in implementing those applications in classrooms. "We have a selection process where we choose one app to focus on. Then, as an entire class, they research and become experts at using it. We meet with the classroom teachers, schedule the time it will take, take the equipment to them, set it up, and work side by side with students in the activity". Through this experience, Kaser's students evaluate software, become technology mentors, and reinforce their own understanding of the content in the applications.

In late 2016 these ideas were just scribbles on Kaser's yellow notepad. As a high school technology teacher, David has a fair amount of latitude in the type of classes he teaches, and he envisioned a class about virtual reality in education. The biggest barrier, as for many educators, was the money involved in purchasing the equipment. He wrote grants to Arconic and obtained a grant to fund a large part of the purchase, and received additional funding from a local foundation, Barberton Community Foundation, and PPG. "When the grant application process was going through we didn't have the equipment so I couldn't say 'come in and see it'. Now we have the equipment, and people can come into the lab and try it out. When visitors come in, I have the students work with them. The students set them up in the headset, and talk them through the basic controls. It's good practice for the students". David traveled with his class of students and the equipment to the Ohio Ed Tech Conference (OETC) to introduce other teachers to the applications and idea of using VR in their classrooms. Kaser explains, "We presented what we have done and how we set it up – each setup had a different educational application running in to the headset. I also want to have students research different VR technologies – Samsung, Google cardboard, Vive, so they can share that information with different teachers. The students are excited to be a part of it".

Realistic Virtual Reality

These three examples provide some insight into how to infuse virtual reality realistic for the classroom. In some cases, students bring their own phones and the school supplies the headsets, in others devices are shared district wide from a central office or even housed in a classroom and shared across schools. Finding ways to transport and charge devices between classes can involve retrofitting existing backpacks or modifying photography or audiovisual equipment. Teachers can find support from administrators, parents, or involve students as tech support in their classrooms. Teachers, administrators, and schools can help find and evaluate educational applications. In the second half of this book educator David Kaser will describe his approach in developing and sustaining a VR lab at his high school in Barberton, Ohio. In the final chapter, his students share their feedback from their experiences with VR.

At MIT, we are developing virtual reality applications that can are feasible in today's classrooms but also push the boundaries of educational VR applications. The MIT Education Arcade and MIT Game Lab are currently working on Collaborative Learning Environments in Virtual Reality, or CLEVR (https://education.mit.edu/project/clevr/). CLEVR is an interactive, immersive game where introductory biology students work together to learn about cellular biology and the central dogma (DNA to RNA to protein) in order to diagnose a problem in a cell. Through designing the game, we are also investigating how to create virtual reality environments that can be interactive, collaborative, and can enable students to incorporate their own designs and creativity. We are talking with cell biologists and medical experts to create an authentic environment. CLEVR is informative, fun, and leverages virtual reality's ability to transport students to a place that is otherwise impossible to experience: the inside of a human cell.

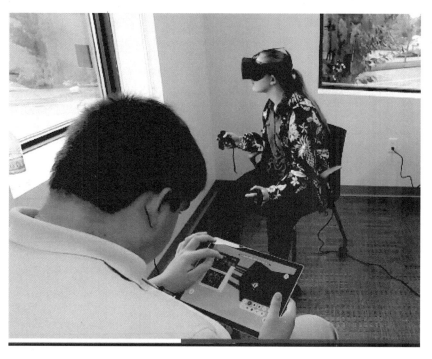

Cellverse is a two person game designed to emphasize communication and teamwork

Current uses and resources for VR focus on individual experiences with limited interactivity such as virtual field trips and guided tours. While sensory immersion can be powerful, these uses do not capitalize on the power of the medium. The next steps in 3D immersive VR in the classroom should draw upon the ability for students to explore spatial relationships such as architectural designs and chemical structures, to involve local and remote learners to collaborate, and to enable students to integrate different types of data (graphs, charts, and 3D models) in meaningful ways (Hew & Chung, 2010; Dede, in press;). Immersive 3DVR has the potential to change how students engage with those topics, and large-scale implementation of 3D immersive VR scale should capitalize on how this medium can push the boundaries of learning in new dimensions.

Note that a previous version of the article appeared in T.H.E. Journal in January 2018. https://thejournal.com/articles/2018/01/11/making-virtual-reality-a-reality-in-todays-classrooms.aspx

References

Bolkan, J. (2017, December 04). Virtual and Augmented Reality to Nearly Double Each Year Through 2021. Retrieved December 07, 2017, from https://thejournal.com/articles/2017/12/04/virtual-and-augmented-reality-to-nearly double-each-year-through-2021.aspx

Castaneda, L., Cechony, A., Bautista A.. (2017) Applied VR in the Schools, 2016-2017 Aggregated Report. Foundry 10. Accessed 12/1/17. http://foundry10.org/wp-content/uploads/2017/09/All-School-Aggregated-Findings-2016-2017.pdf

Dede, C. (in press). Introduction: Virtual, augmented, and mixed realities in education. in Dede, C. (ed) *The 60-Year Curriculum: New Models for Lifelong Learning in the Digital Economy*. London, U.K. Routledge, U.K..

Hew, K. F., & Cheung, W. S. (2010). Use of three-dimensional (3-D) immersive virtual worlds in K-12 and higher education settings: A review of the research. *British Journal of Educational Technology*, 41(1), 33–55. http://doi.org/10.1111/j.14678535.2008.00900.x

Zimmerman, E. (March 2019). K-12 Teachers Use Augmented and Virtual Reality Platforms to Teach Biology. *EdTech focus on K12.* https://edtechmagazine.com/k12/article/2019/03/k-12-teachers-use-augmented-and-virtual-reality-platforms-teach-biology-perfcon Accessed September 4, 2019.

3

IMAGINING VR FOR EDUCATION IN THE DEVELOPING WORLD

Over the past few years, virtual reality (VR) has begun to rapidly expand in capabilities and availability, and simultaneously decreasing in costs and limitations. The lower cost and increased access has resulted in discussion about how, and where, to incorporate VR into learning environments. As a result, school administrators, teachers, and non-profits are beginning to explore the potential of VR in the classroom (Castaneda, Cechony & Bautista, 2017; Thompson, 2018).

However, this discussion rarely focuses on equity, especially across countries in the global south. The movement to increase global equity in education requires us to consider how students in every learning environment can make use of new technologies, even in light of perceived challenges. This paper explores this emerging landscape of VR as a tool for schools and local education organizations operating in low-resource settings. We explore the core requirements necessary for success, some of the key risks to consider for thoughtful implementation, and possible uses in coming years.

Current research shows that VR holds promise as an educational resource due to its promise for embodied learning: creating a convincing, interactive, user-controlled world that provides rich opportunities to spark learning (Bailey & Bailenson, 2017). As the conversation over VR in education grows, allowing it to diffuse into education contexts with readily available funding only reinforces inequality of learning opportunities. "Despite challenges, VR's expansion into classrooms and homes in developed countries, necessitates that learners, everywhere, are considered for equity of access and for the potential learning gains that can take place," says Vikas Pota, Chief Executive of Tmrw Digital. EdTech has the potential to change the game and play a vital role in plugging the gap between developing nations and their counterparts" (Vikas Pota, personal communication, October 2018).

As a result, we are interested in sharing stories and ideas from early adopters of VR in low resource settings. We interviewed people who have insight into making it work, highlighting both the excitement and realism of expanding global access to VR from early adopters.

As the technology is still novel to many individuals, we will define its components briefly here. VR can be broken down into three parts: 1) something you look through (a headset), 2) something you look at (the content), and 3) something that allows those two parts to work together (the connection). The defining feature of VR is the user's ability to interact with a new immersive environment, creating an experience in which the real world is occluded and the user is able to experience an endless spectrum of worlds in first person (Kiefer & Trumpp, 2012). VR typically features an individual wearing a headset viewing a three-dimensional image. The headset's display is connected to a motion sensor that adjusts the user's image based on their head movements in real time, giving the user the sensation of looking around and surveying a virtual landscape. Sometimes, the headset also provides associated sounds, and even haptic feedback. Combined, the student is provided with an immersive environment reactive to their movements and decisions, and one in they enter into a learning scenario first-hand (Dede, in press; Hew & Cheung, 2010).

Even though there are significant barriers, early adopter educators in low resource settings are interested in the ability to use embodied learning to shape meaningful, contextually relevant learning experiences. In VR, students in Dakar can virtually travel through Senegal's Jolof empire, navigating through the pre-colonial landscape from a first-person perspective. Aspiring doctors in Laos can be transported inside the human body where they can practice surgical outcomes, simultaneously saving resources and removing risk to human life. A diverse group of students in Lebanon can helm a virtual ship, learning the importance of dialogue and joint decision-making through an immersive simulation.

For all of these scenarios, VR provides visual, visceral feedback that enhances learning outcomes. As VR expert, Dave Lockwood, a South African VR expert with Naledi3d Factory, points out, virtual reality removes barriers in comprehension that can often occur with traditional textbook learning. In many low-resource education settings, language barriers create challenging contexts where students may not be learning in their native language, teachers may not be teaching in their preferred language, and textbooks and materials may not be provided in a language in which either the teacher or student are proficient. VR overcomes language as a barrier by turning content visual, leveling the linguistic environment and creating a universal experience (Lockwood, 2004; Lockwood 2019). "Concepts such as plate tectonics or the first law of motion can be made visual, giving the learner a mental framework and context, equivalent to making the textbook into a novel" (Lockwood, personal communication, 2018). Furthermore, besides simply guiding students through the material, VR can assist in real-time assessment, capturing where the student may struggle or need more time, particularly when learners are attempting to master complex, often abstract, concepts, especially common in mathematics and the sciences (Lockwood, 2004; Lockwood, 2019).

For students in developing school settings, VR holds transformative possibilities by acting as a stand-in for unavailable resources, materials, or staff. Due to its reusability and potential array of content choices, a high school science lab without equipment or materials can use a shared VR headset to help students virtually control chemical reactions. VR can also help special educators work with neuro-diverse learners students with anxiety, depression or trauma, as well as to develop social-emotional learning skills through its prowess in immersive empathy-based storytelling.

Classroom awaiting students before the start of the school day in Nanton, Ghana.

Overcoming Barriers

As a relatively recent technology, VR has been slow to gain traction and widely penetrate the school landscape. VR remains challenging for teachers to implement in high resource settings. It may, therefore, appear almost impossible for use with learners in lower resource contexts. Significant barriers exist for utilizing VR in learning environments where multiple critical priorities compete with limited time, staff and funds. However, we believe that technology access will continue to expand over time, similar to the growth of smartphones across the globe. Educators can be served by an awareness of the changing landscape and the options available for new learning tools as the availability and options continue to evolve. At present, mid-range VR headsets are available for less than the price of high-end smartphones. The market is expected to continue expanding and improving in the coming years, potentially rendering VR an affordable option for classrooms around the world (Brown & Green, 2016). As VR spreads, we can learn from those who are overcoming these barriers, in turn helping those who may wish to do the same now or in the future.

For this article, we spoke with 7 technologists, including international early adopters, EdTech leaders and non-profit technology managers, to learn what their experience could teach about implementing VR for education in low resource settings. The following recommendations are intended to guide schools, teams, and programs in critical considerations for incorporating VR.

1. Focus on the Learning Goals First

New technology often brings with it new excitement and visions of innovative frontiers. For leaders interested in seizing new opportunities, this excitement can easily overwhelm other motivations, including the intended educational impact. However, when evaluating the potential for using VR in areas where resources are scarce, it is imperative that technology use is never the primary goal in itself. Instead, authentic engagement puts the learning outcomes first and the technology choices second (Kolb, 2017). Once the specific goal for student development has been set, then the spectrum of possible instructional and technology solutions can be explored, including comparing the costs of equipment and training.

2. Match Learning Goals with Appropriate Technology

Once VR has been determined as the best solution for the learning challenge at hand, the question turns to what type of hardware to use and which options are most feasible for the context's strengths and challenges. The range of VR options has become incredibly diverse. However, the choice of hardware can have significant impact on the success of the program, as is detailed in the second half of this book. While the sticker price of hardware options is an immediate concern, more factors flow into the final cost of a system and will affect the difficulties a team will encounter in a low-resource setting. Some options require the purchase of computers to power the headset, which frequently have costly minimum performance requirements. Systems designed for higher resolutions will require more bandwidth and a higher-end computer. Furthermore, the durability of the components will determine the frequency with which they need to be replaced, thereby affecting both the yearly maintenance cost and the effort involved. For example, headsets that are on the far low end in cost may break after repeated handling, but are more easily replaceable. On the other end of the spectrum are expensive systems requiring elaborate wiring harnesses, physical maintenance and security protocols. More complex types of VR systems also come with more complexity in configuring the VR experience for students, particularly in the number of units able to be purchased and operated at the same time. Therefore, considering the impact of hardware decisions on instructional design, exploring the options and understanding the range of implications at the outset can set a VR program up for success. It is recommended to explore options in person, physically test them and get comfortable with the range of tools directly, continually incorporating what works best for the given context and its challenges.

3. Acknowledge Resource Challenges Up front

Successfully deploying VR and associated technologies such as AR in low-resource settings follows a path quite similar to launching a new technology in any environment: teams across all industries and territories may never have the perfect plans, perfect landscape, or perfect facts to implement a vision without facing challenges. However, low-resource education environments do face fundamental difficulties. While the benefits of VR can be attractive, low-resource school environments operate in circumstances where, at initial glance, technology can appear as an overwhelming or even untenable proposition. Resource scarcity brings significant difficulties in funding, personnel time and skill sets, security, and hardware maintenance. Moreover, leaders must work through difficult stakeholder environments, political complexity, and procurement processes that can hamper even the most determined. With already stretched workloads, short-term funding periods, and many existing priorities, school leaders or program teams are unlikely to excitedly wade into VR without support, and may forgo VR in light of more immediate priorities.

Particularly acute is the fact that teams may not be able to rely on infrastructure taken for granted in developed countries. For instance, a desired location may lack stable power and internet connectivity. Many VR solutions require a reliable, high bandwidth connection to a server. "Anything with high latency and high bandwidth is not feasible in many settings," says Daniel Caughlin, Deputy Director of Programs Technology and Product Management for the International Rescue Committee. Furthermore, remote areas may not have support services for long-term maintenance or ongoing training. Many of the VR solutions are delicate and sensitive to dust. Without a safe place to store the equipment, it can quickly degrade.

For teams who have determined that VR is the right solution for their learners' needs, overcoming these challenges requires a dedicated change of mindset and often a change of timeline. Teams must acknowledge and embrace the difficulties they may encounter, and then tackle unexpected setbacks or tasks one by one. Continued problem solving and learning become the key component in the path towards success. By embracing the setting and the challenges at the forefront, teams can continually generate momentum for finding solutions. Dave Lockwood shared, for example, that while planning for a deployment in South Africa, the Department of Education nearly refused to entertain his team's idea of AR/VR. Many of the country's schools lack textbooks and officials therefore viewed VR as an unnecessary luxury. Lockwood, however, was not deterred in helping convince government leaders of VR's potential for replacing textbooks themselves. He notes that,

"It's always easier to find reasons why not to do something. Instead, find solutions to the problems and execute on those plans. When we were faced with internet connectivity problems, for instance, we put the content onto a local hard drive. We made it work. If we all wait for external infrastructure to make these projects easy, the world will look the same in 50 years. Instead, just do it. You can figure it out. The more examples that are available in these regions, the more others will consider it for themselves and their own problems."

4. Start with and support a single champion

When deploying VR for the first time, begin with a small, low-stakes trial via a local champion. In low-resource settings, VR is likely an unknown technology, and there may be limited prior exposure. Often, the best way to begin is through finding an individual who is personally convinced of the project's benefits, who has the willingness to problem-solve, and who is committed to making the project succeed. This person could be a single teacher in the school, a single official in the Ministry of Education or a single program leader who is excited and can act as champion for the project throughout its lifespan.

For many schools and non-profit programs in developing settings, staff are extremely under-resourced and many may not see themselves as technology-inclined. A good local champion will recognize the value proposition, be passionate about helping the vision succeed, and be willing to invest their own time and efforts in supporting the project. Moreover, an ideal champion will be someone who is a little technologically savvy, or at the very least someone who excited by the technology and who has the energy and confidence to work through the unknowns (Lockwood, personal communication, October 2018). Once this champion is found, they are a valuable resource throughout the entire launch process – from design to scale up. Not only can a champion help ensure designs match reality, but if their feedback and needs are successfully included within the project, they will advocate for the program's expansion and provide support to other early adopters, letting their enthusiasm radiate once the project is running.

For example, a single educator who is excited by VR's use for an instructional outcome may be willing to give it a try in their classroom. Rolling VR in one educator's classroom out as a mini-pilot will reveal the types of resources needed and potential barriers to using VR in that school. The teacher may find, for instance, that the space available in a classroom is insufficient, or the charging facilities require more secure storage options. These challenges become opportunities for educators and even students to design carrying cases as David Kaser describes in chapter 3 of this book, and charging options as Chris Turner discusses in chapter 1 of this book. As the system is tested, other teachers and staff will have the chance to hear about and see the system in use. If the VR experience is useful and going well, word will spread and interest will build, creating the buy-in to expand the system.

5. Let people get their hands on it

As stated, VR can be intimidating for newcomers. Any VR project needs to take this trepidation into account and provide a relaxed, non-committal path for newcomers, to become comfortable with it. The most effective tool for reducing and eliminating fear is exposure. As a program launches and scales, allowing people to touch it, practice with it, and see it in use – without any commitment – will help to demystify the technology, spread better understanding of the idea's merit, and provide role models for newcomers.

6. Plan Classroom Dynamics

Incorporating VR into an educational setting requires thoughtful consideration to the holistic experience of learners, teachers and their classroom interactions. Alongside a champion and initial users, classroom dynamics must be planned out. Interactions between students and teachers, or even student to student, are often fundamental to the broader learning taking place. Launching a VR program, therefore, must keep in mind how learners will use the headset, how teachers or external staff will support them or teach alongside, and how this new tool will shape the instructional design choices of the wider lesson.

In South Africa, for instance, Naledi3d Factory developed and deployed a "Virtual Trainer" now in use in rural, government schools. This Augmented Reality (AR) system facilitates modeling of complex academic concepts, designed for a teacher to lead as a whole-class lesson, as they had traditionally done. However, rather than guiding students through pages of a textbook, the teacher selects objects from a virtual 'library' for students to then personally combine and manipulate within their headsets. The teacher places a virtual human cell into the students' view and then guides students through 'unpacking' each component part. Used alongside supplemental text and video clips, the teacher guides students through a virtual 'hands-on' learning session. In both of these scenarios, the traditional teacher-led learning environment is enhanced by providing the opportunity for embodied learning where "learners can now choose, explore, manipulate, test and make transformations within objects and ideas", especially as traditional materials had previously been unavailable (Lockwood, 2004).

In many settings, providing enough headsets to cover each student in a class simultaneously may not be financially or logistically feasible. Core questions then include how to divide an instructor's time and ensure all students have access, especially given that many school environments in developing nations already face challenges of overcrowding and teaching styles that are often unaccustomed to student 'stations' or small group work. Therefore as program's work through these instructional decisions, some options to consider may include:

- One headset per class: One learner at a time is invited to engage in a relatively brief VR experience, with students taking turns over multiple classroom sessions or days.

- Small groups: A small subset of students (5 or 6) engage in a VR experience while the remainder of the students continue with regular classroom lessons. With this format, it is critical for a separate adult to be available to support these small groups while other students are still with the teacher (Thompson, 2018).

- Outside of class: Create an after-school session that allows a small group of students to engage with the device(s). Rotate the students that join for each session.

- Pairs: Place students in pairs, with one student in each pair actively using a VR device. The other student can follow the experience on a regular screen. Students trade places on a regular basis.

Elementary school classroom in Nanton, Ghana.

7. Stay local

Local Buy-In

A central factor in the success of educational VR in low-resource areas is a team's ability to maintain focus as a program for, and with, the local community. From the outset, a VR project can only succeed in the long-term if teams are able to prioritize getting buy-in from key community stakeholders early on, prior to making any decisions. While it may slow down timelines initially, having key decision makers onboard, such as school and district officials, the

Ministry of Education, or parent groups, will improve long-term sustainability of the program as it launches and scales. Including these stakeholders in ongoing conversations will allow the program to be a collaborative, iterative process. As a result, new local champions may come onboard as successes build, opportunities may expand for establishing important partnerships, and teams may be buffered from hitting blocks in necessary approvals.

Local Suppliers and Locally Targeted Content

Furthermore, the benefits of staying local extends to hardware and content. If at all possible, hardware should be bought from local, reputable suppliers. Importing devices from abroad can unexpectedly create difficulties for those who manage them locally, including for warranties and replacement issues. Instead, local vendors can help support the program more rapidly when in need, as well as more sustainably in the long-term. This approach also helps promote local economies and improves the supply of technology within the community.

Local Content

Beyond the hardware, VR's impact for learners is directly tied to the content of the lessons. While this may appear obvious, the language and cultural context of the content must match the context of the students and needs of local teachers (Lockwood, 2004; Kerawalla, Luckin, Seljeflot & Woolard, 2006). In both high and low-income countries local startups, developers, and organizations are creating locally designed technology solutions for use in local markets. VR production companies and labs have sprung up worldwide, including in Estonia, the Ukraine, India,

Nairobi, Lagos, South Africa, and Dhaka (Lockwood, 2019; Mitter, 2018; Morris, Lowe, & Crous, 2010; Todavchych, 2019). Utilizing these providers to create localized content, including culturally and ethnically relevant visuals, enables greater educational experiences. Supporting local or regional content providers also ensures that the development process can be iterative with local end-users, such as teachers and students, who can test versions along the way.

Local Support Staff

Because VR depends so heavily on hardware, remote support may not be sufficient, available, or convenient. With that in mind, teams will want to ensure that staff have dedicated local support, including a local primary "point person" who is fully responsible for the program across any and all sites. This point person serves as a trusted partner and supervisor to seek out regular performance feedback from everyone involved, develop trusting relationships with participants, travel to program sites on a regular basis, put in place controls and processes, and be available for any needed re-trainings or support.

8. Consider Equity, Inclusion and Protection

The rise of VR, like any edtech endeavor, presents an opportunity for deep conversations around equity, inclusion, and diversity. In the drive for education outcomes, few content developers have engaged in deep considerations around how their technology interplays with issues of gender parity, socio-economic disparities, and protection or access rights for potential users. In many contexts, education initiatives – from school access to teaching quality – operate within long-standing issues of equity between students or between communities. New VR programs should be deeply considerate of these dynamics. Program staff need to consider gender, inclusion, and protection dynamics of technology use: who owns it, who gets access to it and who does not, and how everyone's basic dignities are upheld in the process. For example, are females and males provided equal access; do students or teachers face threats, exploitation or abuse as a result of their access to an expensive new tool; are learners with special needs included in the program?

9. Make plans for long-term use

As with any technology project, VR and AR devices will, at some point, encounter technical difficulties. Programs and staff will also change and evolve. Incorporating long-term technical management in your initial planning will help avoid surprises as well as devices going unmaintained in a closet. Prior to launching a system, teams will need to have both long-term budgets and human resources for managing software updates, troubleshooting support, maintaining hardware and creating process controls that can adapt to change.

For instance, software updates, and the connectivity and bandwidth to install them, can be an easily overlooked impediment that catches teams unprepared. On the hardware front, all devices eventually have issues or break, especially within the hands of students. A technical plan therefore needs to include how often devices are brought into internet connectivity, if spare devices are purchased and available, who is in charge of in-person troubleshooting, how losses are handled, and how devices are repaired. Similar to having an ongoing point-person, all teams are well-served by having someone specifically trained and responsible for solving simple technical problems. However, their abilities to solve complex problems, including repairing or replacing equipment, has a limit. The project will need to develop a centralized tech support system that provides a backup when bigger problems exceed their abilities, and a pre-established communication pathway for users to reach out for help.

10. It's okay to have fun!

People everywhere make use of what is entertaining. Mobile phones are popular not for their sole ability to read email and find weather forecasts, but also for their ability to connect to friends and entertainment. Similarly for VR, while the primary aim may be to deliver educational content, do not hesitate to let the content be enjoyable. In Zimbabwe, for example, a project of Naledi3d Factory using Android phones was intended to teach farmers new agricultural practices (Lockwood, 2019). However, the phones also had the ability to record, and people started recording themselves singing. The songs were shared around the village, creating entertainment for everyone and increasing the excitement surrounding the use of the phones for their primary purpose as well (Lockwood, personal communication, October 2018).

Next Steps

As we have explored, VR is not a simple solution, particularly for education in the developing world. Challenges may be immense and continuous, even for the most motivated of teams. However, for those who are ready to embrace the challenge, benefits may also be sizable for the learner directly, as well as in accelerating the equitable distribution of technology between and amongst settings. For those inspired by emerging opportunities and the possibilities of innovation, the recommendations presented here may serve as a reminder that success is possible.

As the educational VR industry develops and grows, further investigation will be needed. Continued research will be helpful in illuminating more of the inputs required to successfully, and more easily deploying VR in low-resource education environments, as well as the long-term impacts on target student populations. At present, the impact of VR use on young children requires further investigation, especially the effects of solitary learning and understanding of virtual versus real worlds (Bailey & Bailenson, 2017). Further research will also help broaden collective understanding about VR's short and long-term effects on teachers and teaching, and on school environments as a whole.

References

Bailey, J. O., & Bailenson, J. N. (2017). Considering virtual reality in children's lives. *Journal of Children and Media*, 11(1), 107-113.

Brown, A., & Green, T. (2016). Virtual Reality: Low-Cost Tools and Resources for the Classroom. *TechTrends*, 60(5), 517-519.

Castaneda, L. M., Bindman, S. W., Cechony, A., & Sidhu, M. (2018). The disconnect between real and virtually real worlds: The challenges of using VR with adolescents. *PRESENCE: Teleoperators and Virtual Environments*, 26(4), 453-453.

Dede, C. (in press). Introduction: Virtual, augmented, and mixed realities in education. in Dede, C. (ed) *The 60-Year Curriculum: New Models for Lifelong Learning in the Digital Economy*. London, U.K. Routledge, U.K..

Hew, K. F., & Cheung, W. S. (2010). Use of three-dimensional (3-D) immersive virtual worlds in K-12 and higher education settings: A review of the research. *British Journal of Educational Technology*, 41(1), 33–55. http://doi.org/10.1111/j.1467-8535.2008.00900.

Kerawalla, L, Luckin, R., Seljeflot, S., & Woolard, A. (2006) Making it real: exploring the potential of augmented reality for teaching primary school science. *Virtual Reality, 10(3-4), 163-174.*

Kiefer, M.T, and Trumpp, M.N (2012). Embodiment theory and education: the foundations of cognition in perception and action. *Trends in Neuroscience Education.* 1,15–20. doi: 10.1016/j.tine.2012.07.002.

Kolb, L. (2017). *Learning First, Technology Second: The Educator's Guide to Designing Authentic Lessons*. International Society for Technology in Education.

Lockwood, D. (1999). *Evaluation of virtual reality in Africa: an educational perspective.* UNESCO. Retrieved from: http://unesdoc.unesco.org/images/0013/001346/134 607e.pdf.

Lockwood, D. (2019). the Nalidi3d Factory website. http://www.naledi3d.com/ Accessed September 4, 2019.

Mitter, S. (June, 2018). 5 cutting-edge virtual reality startups in

India to watch out for. *Your Story.* https://yourstory.com/2018/06/ 5-cutting-edge-virtual-reality-startups-india-watch. Accessed September 4, 2019.

Morris, L. D., Louw, Q. A., & Crous, L. C. (2010). Feasibility and potential effect of a low-cost virtual reality system on reducing pain and anxiety in adult burn injury patients during physiotherapy in a developing country. *Burns, 36(5),* 659-664.

Tan, S., and Waugh, R. (2014). "Use of virtual-reality in teaching and learning molecular biology," in *3D Immersive and Interactive Learning,* ed Y. Kai (Amsterdam: IOS Press), 17–43.

Todavchych, J. (2019). To Virtual Reality Companies in 2019. ThinkMobile. https://thinkmobiles.com/blog/virtual-reality-companies/ Accessed September 4 2019.

Thompson, M. M., Wang, A., Roy, D., & Klopfer, E. (2018). Authenticity, Interactivity, and Collaboration in VR learning games. *Frontiers in Robotics and AI,* 5,133.

Thompson, M. (2018). Making Virtual Reality a Reality in Today's Classrooms. *THE Journal. Retrieved from* https://thejournal.com/ articles/2018/01/11/making-virtual -reality-a-reality-in-todays-classrooms.aspx

Also included in the study:

- *Interview with Daniel Caughlin*

- *Interview with Mona Akmal (VR for neuro-diverse learners)*

- *Interview with Embodied Labs (let people get their hands on it)*

- *Interview with Vikas Pota, Varkey Foundation*

Part II

The "How To's" of VR Integration

4

THREE LEVELS OF VR INTEGRATION

David Kaser and Meredith Thompson

Overview

The technology behind virtual reality has long been dreamed of in sci-fi. Movies like "Lawnmower Man," "Hackers," "Johnny Mnemonic", and "Ready Player One" foresaw a world where users would don a headset and travel into a virtual world. Welcome to where sci-fi is finally realized.

The applications of virtual reality are extensive: military training, industrial machine training, surgical training, gaming. But what about education? VR has its place in education also, but research and planning are necessary to make it successful.

We will take a look at three levels of VR integration in education. Each one has its place in education and depends on a variety of factors, such as budget, target grade levels, physical space, and technology comfort levels of staff. We understand that even though the technology will change, the examples illustrated in the examples below can be applied to a multitude of educational settings.

*Note that all prices are accurate as of September 2019.

Jet-Setting Around the World

Description:

This level of VR is fantastic for lower grades and/or entry level experiences. Note that VR is not currently recommended for children under the age of 13.

Equipment Choices:

- The most inexpensive choice for technology is Google Cardboard. The drawback with this option is the need for each student to have their own smart device with the needed apps downloaded.

- Oculus Go is a stand-alone device with a two button remote for menu selection capabilities.

- Google Expedition Kits – sold in kits of 10, 20, or 30.

- Oculus Quest.

What does it look like within a classroom?

Lessons, mostly virtual field trips, can be designed to take students to far off lands. The Google Expedition kits are easy to pass from teacher to teacher and classroom to classroom. Teachers do not need much training to get this type VR up and running.

Entry level cost:

- Amazon offers Google cardboard for $25/2-pack*.

- Oculus Go has a starting price of $200* for the 32 GB model.

- Google Expedition kits can be purchased through Best Buy and cost $4000/$6700/$9400* for the kits of 10/20/30, respectively.

- Oculus Quest has an entry price of $399* for the 64GB model.

Using a Google Expedition kit or Google Cardboard allows students to remain at a desk and does not require room to move around.

Interactive 3D VR....on a Budget

Description:

If you want to have access to the most interactive VR experiences and equipment on the market, but resources are limited, then this plan is for you. The equipment and available content is best suited for grades 7-12.

Equipment Choices*:

The three primary choices in this category are the Oculus Rift S, Oculus Quest, HTC Vive, Vive Cosmos, and Windows Mixed Reality. The base price for these devices is $400-$500* plus gaming computers are required for some models ($1300-$1500* each).

What does it look like within a classroom?

There are two effective options for this level of implementation. One is a permanent location such as a library or media center where 2-4 VR stations would be set up and managed by the media center specialist. Classes would come in and use it. The second option is a mobile system where a technology leader would come in and set up the equipment in the back of a classroom for the duration of the lesson. In both cases, the VR app would be used as a station within a larger framework. A teacher would devise a lesson, involving multiple learning styles and activities, including the VR experience as one activity. Students would rotate through each station. The duration of these lessons would likely be in the 3-5 day range and require a variety of activities to engage all students at all times.

Entry level cost:

Each station, a VR equipment and a gaming computer, will have a base price around $2000*. For a class of 25 students, three or four VR sets would be needed to make it an effective station within an educational lesson.

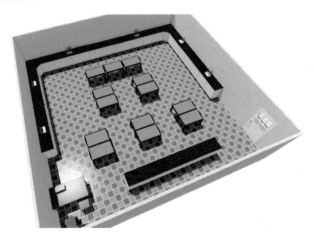

This shows a physical layout designed for a limited number of VR stations around the perimeter. The remaining area is set-up for student groups to work at other stations.

The VR World is our Playground

Description:

This level of VR taps into the most interactive level of VR experiences. The equipment and available content is best suited for grades 7-12.

Equipment Choices*:

Your equipment choices are the same as the last category. The three primary choices in this category are the Oculus Rift S, HTC Vive, Vive Cosmos, and Windows Mixed Reality. The base price for these devices is $400-$500*.

What does it look like within a classroom?

This level of commitment to incorporate VR into education creates a dynamic environment of student interactivity with technology and other students. One possible classroom design would involve creating a class where students are trained to evaluate content, create lessons, and utilize their expertise to become VR assistants within a classroom. These trained students set up the equipment and remain in the classroom to help with the implementation of the equipment and troubleshoot issues that arise to keep the lesson running smoothly. This classroom model empowers the students and relieves the classroom teacher from having to learn how to set up, troubleshoot, and operate the equipment. This set up affords them the freedom to interact with their students and check for understanding.

Entry level cost:

Each station, VR equipment and a gaming computer, will have a base price around $2000*. We recommend 15 headsets for a class of 25-30 students and 20 headsets for a class of 35 students to maximize student involvement.

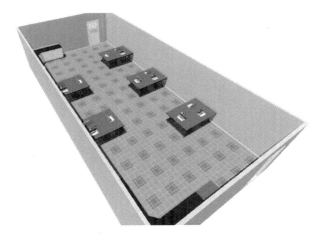

The layout demonstrates a possible arrangement using 15 VR stations where students work in pairs. We use a similar setup when my VR team works with other classes. We position one student from my class who is the "VR expert" during the class at every pod.

Making a Plan

Once you have an idea of the systems and scope, the next step is to make a plan. Consider your overall educational goals, for example, establish a strategy to ensure you and your fellow educators find and share high quality VR resources. How will these resources be used? Purchasing a classroom set of equipment is expensive. Ask if your educational goals can be met by having a smaller set of devices and setting up stations in the classroom. Once your educational goals are set, then determine how many devices you will purchase in order to meet those educational needs.

Another consideration is technology management. Who will be in charge of the equipment? Who will troubleshoot when the technology is not working properly? How will teachers become familiar with VR and how best to use VR in the classroom? Here our own students may be valuable resources. Some schools have students as "tech support". Perhaps the students could set up a workshop for the teachers on how to use VR.

We present some possible ways to address these issues in the following chapters.

5

VR IN K12

Building a Program from the Ground Up

David Kaser and Meredith Thompson

INTRODUCTION

Virtual reality (VR) is coming to education. The costs are falling and educational opportunities are expanding. What is it like to begin with nothing and create a program to maximize the potential of VR technology? We will take a look at how one high school is attempting to make the most of their investment and enhance student learning through an innovative approach to education.

A Brief Distinction Between VR Types

A quick Google search for resources associated with VR and a person will see the results are a bit confusing. To simplify things for the sake of discussion, we will group types into two main categories: Mobile VR (such as Google Cardboard or Samsung GearVR) and Interactive 3D VR. Mobile VR is the cheapest and simplest form, and is a great starting point for schools new to the game or with a limited budget. Generally, using mobile VR includes Google Expeditions and 360 degree videos. In a narrative VR setting, the user is being taken on a tour and is unable to interact or control the story. The Samsung GearVR provides the user with a limited amount of interaction and navigation, but lacks the ability to truly interact with their environment. They are able to make selections within the VR environment but unable to create. Interactive 3D VR allows the user to interact with their environment, make changes, and dictate the pace of information/play.

This chapter illustrates how one high school in Ohio sought to create a class that uses interactive 3D VR to enhance education and provide a framework for how other schools could duplicate the process.

Where to Begin

Before a single dollar is spent, a decision needs to be made about the overarching goals of the program. Realistically, the ability to meet goals is linked to the available resources. Some questions that need to be answered include:

- What is the purpose of the class? What will the students gain besides free access to VR?

- What type of VR will be used?

- What is the purpose of the equipment?

  - Provide a mobile kit to be signed out by classroom teachers and be used for Google Expeditions, virtual field trips, and 360° videos.

  - Create a class for students to learn about VR and play games in a singular location.

  - Explore the educational applications of interactive 3D VR and implement it in traditional classroom settings.

- Who will oversee the class/equipment? (hint: choose an organized person)

VR Type Dictates the Equipment

If your goal is to create a mobile virtual field trip, there are options available to purchase pre-assembled kits. If you are ambitious and have the available funding and want to go all-in with an interactive 3D VR lab, mobile or "permanent", then you will need to do your research. VR systems like the Oculus Rift S and HTC Vive need gaming computers with high-end graphics cards and sufficient RAM to handle the visual aspects of the experiences. While choosing interactive VR and gaming computers drives the cost up considerably, the potential educational gains are significant.

Peripheral Products You Didn't Consider, but You Should

We have learned many things throughout our journey of creating an interactive 3D VR mobile lab. Some things we planned on and some things were a surprise. We'll start with a list of "optional" products that need to be considered – lessons we learned along the way.

- Multiple users? – Oculus face masks are a sponge-like material that absorb sweat. Purchase replacement face masks from a third party provider with a less porous material.

- Anti-bacterial wipes (individual packets) – to wipe down face masks between users.

- Defogging wipes (individual packets) – cleans lenses and helps prevent fogging.

- Microfiber clothes – handy for wiping lenses off on the go.

- Batteries – have a supply on hand to replace hand

controller batteries.

- Powerstrips – if you are using laptops and are mobile, these are a necessity.

- Power cords – if you are using laptops and charge them in a cart, these are a must. These make it easier to set-up and tear-down equipment without rebuilding the back end of a laptop cart each time.

- Gamepads/VR Remotes – some VR experiences do not use the VR controllers and require gamepads or another device, such as a special remote.

- Mirrors – Allowing students to check their appearance after emerging from VR, which can be important for students.

- Anti-nausea preparations – Water, ginger candy, and peppermints may help allieviate nausea. We recommend keeping those supplies on hand (Johnson, 2017).

LOGISTICS

Who's in charge?

This might be the most important question that needs to be answered. The two key people include the district technology leader and the teacher who will oversee the program. The district tech person will need to allow the VR computers to bypass the district filtering system and set-up email aliases for each Oculus/ Viveport/STEAM account needed (one per computer).

How do you purchase new apps/experiences?

The Oculus store and STEAM are run similarly to Apple's App Store or Google Play, and both of these platforms need access to a credit card. Good luck getting access to the district credit card. One solution is using gift cards (such as Visa gift cards), allowing the instructor to approve and oversee each purchase. Using this approach reduces the likelihood a student will purchase VR experiences that are inappropriate for school.

Who is responsible for software updates?

This is a fairly simple issue and depends on who oversees the program. If a class is specifically designed to explore VR applications, then each pair of students can be assigned to a computer. Any time updates need to be installed, they are in charge of handling it. This promotes student responsibility and ownership while cutting down on the workload for the instructor. If the equipment is under the oversight of a staff member, then he or she would handle any updates.

Equipment Organization

Organizing, labeling, and documenting all of the equipment is a tedious task that needs to be handled before ever hitting the first power button. The technology used in VR must be paired with the computer. Being consistent with the VR equipment and computer partnerships cuts down on future configuration time and confusion. We use a simple numbering system (VR-1 to VR-15) and label each piece using a metallic Sharpie marker.

Storage of the equipment depends on the physical logistics. If you have permanent physical space, much of the equipment can be left set-up at all times. Being mobile created a need for VR backpacks, a cart to store the backpacks, and a laptop cart.

Each VR set and laptop is numbered and always paired. Consistency and organization increases efficiency.

A Synopsis of the Barberton VR Class

All of these lessons were learned through the experience of creating and implementing a VR lab for high school students. Here is an overview of the class, demographics and equipment:

- Number of classes: 1

- Number of students: 19

- Age of students: Grades 10-12

- Class format: Year-long elective course that meets 48 minutes every day

- School Demographics: Suburban, free/reduced lunch is above 70%

- Equipment: 15 Oculus Rifts with Touch controllers

- Computers: HP Omen laptops

- Additional Equipment: Oculus Remotes and Xbox One controllers with Bluetooth

Purpose of the VR class: Our goal is to maximize the return on our investment through training students to become near-peer technology experts. In doing so, our students improved their 21st Century skill set through increases in information literacy, technology literacy, oral and written communication, collaboration, and creativity.

Class Structure: My VR students take part in the educational process from beginning to end. In doing so, they gain valuable skills that are transferable to the real world. Students choose partners to collaborate with all year.

VR Introductory Period: It all begins with students learning to use and care for the equipment. In doing so, we cover vocabulary, concepts, and potential uses of VR in education.

Product/App Research and Evaluation: One focus of the class is student research. Student pairs are given freedom of choice and search for potential VR apps to test. They select one app and spend two or three days testing it, looking for potential educational benefit. The evaluation includes a summary of online user reviews, personal opinion, content standards covered, where it fits in the curriculum, and an overall rating. All of this information is entered into a Google Form. If the app is deemed worthwhile, they move onto the next step.

Information Gathering: The selected app is now purchased for all 15 computers. The class uses Google docs to record all the information/vocabulary/concepts covered in the app.

The VR team works in pairs to gather information and assess VR applications.

Lesson Design: The class decides on pre and post VR experience activities and collectively design a mini-lesson for a traditional classroom to use.

Student/Staff Collaboration: A core content teacher is brought in to demo the VR experience at the direction of a student. Then a small group of students sit down and present the lesson idea/format with the teacher, making changes if needed.

VR Implementation: VR students set up the equipment and take on the role of near-peer technology tutors. They work with the regular classroom students, handle technology issues, and assist the classroom teacher with technology implementation. This frees the content teacher from being responsible for the technology, allowing them to focus on interacting with students around the lesson content.

Assessment of Student Understanding: A VR experience in itself is valuable, but we use a follow-up activity to reinforce concepts/vocabulary and check for knowledge acquisition. Much like everything else we do, this is also student driven. After thoroughly testing an app, the class looks for creative assessment ideas that fit within the topic. It may be free verse poetry using vocabulary, "How Certain Are You?", creating a Twitter board, designing a billboard advertisement, or a humorous "Top 10 List". Students share their ideas and one is chosen to include in the mini-lesson plan. Our goal is to provide the classroom teacher with a method of assessment, while keeping it engaging, allowing for student creativity to shine.

Follow-up: A Google form survey is given to traditional classroom students to collect data and feedback on the performance of the VR students, quality of the VR experience, and appropriateness of the pre- and post-activity.

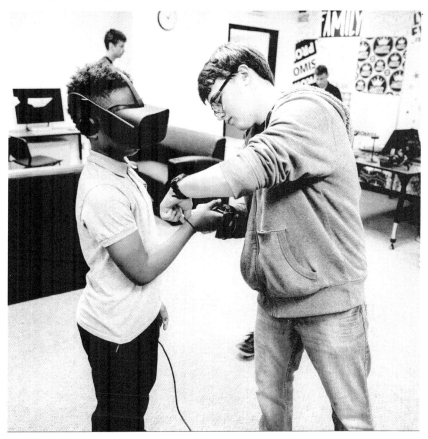

A VR student expert assists a student with any questions or problems they encounter. They handle all technology questions, including setup and tear down.

6

STUDENT VOICE COUNTS

Assessing VR Applications

David Kaser and Meredith Thompson

Yelp. Amazon. Rotten Tomatoes. Zagat. We are all familiar with websites and apps driven by user reviews. Expert reviews are crucial when it comes to specs and performance, but everyday life and decisions on products, hotels, food, and movies are guided by the ratings our peers post online. Unfortunately, some of the reviews need to be approached with skepticism. Are the reviews written by people for hire? Is there political bias? Is user error the basis for a poor review or are there real technical issues? These are all things that need considered when relying on online ratings.

In Barberton, Ohio, I have a class of high school students focused on the educational application of virtual reality (VR). A key aspect of the class is testing apps for educational usefulness. In the following sections, we will take a closer look at the system we use to evaluate and rate VR applications and how they design lessons to be used in a traditional classroom. Here we have four goals: to describe the criteria, the research process, the benefits to the students, and the transformation of these ideas into lessons. I have found that giving students a voice in the direction we travel provides ownership in the class and fosters a sense of pride. This is done by allowing students to choose the applications they want to test, provide feedback on the usefulness of the application, and ultimately, decide if we include it in a mini-lesson. Letting them decide shows them their work is important and that I value their input.

For the purpose of discussion, I will use the term "experience" often. This is used in place of "software application" or "app". We use it synonymously with the other terms because it describes what the user encounters while inside the VR app. It is similar to what a person may describe after visiting a haunted house. They talk about what they saw, felt, or touched. Similarly, a user inside a VR app experiences a variety of visual effects and "feelings".

Ratings – The Categories

Ask two people to describe an identical set of events and you will get two different responses. While not entirely exclusive of each other, details will differ based on personal experience and memory discrepancies, the difference in perception of the same events is known as the "Rashomon Effect" (Alia, 1997). Our goal in this class is to find VR educational applications provide consistent measures, streamline the review process, and get students to produce a systematic, evidence-based review. This required us to establish a specific set of criteria.

We created the measures by pooling our own experiences with applications, games, and virtual reality. During classroom discussions, we settled on 6 categories that are important to the user's experience in the VR application: Motion (Comfort level/ Nausea), Interactivity, Usability, Content, Audio, and Stability. We wanted to capture qualitative comments but also create quantitative, easy to access summaries. To do this, we adopted the familiar "5-star" method of scoring for each category. We then averaged the star rating of the 6 categories to assign each VR application an overall rating.

Motion

Many people experience some sort of motion sickness, whether from car rides, airplanes, or roller coasters. These effects are also present in VR depending on the nature of the experience. A 5-star rating means that the typical user will experience little or no nausea.

Interactivity and Usability

Full interactive 3D VR allows the user to interact with their environment and dictate the course of events; however, some VR experiences are known as "ghost stories", meaning the user is nothing more than an audience member seeing what the developer wants them to see. Apps that have more interactivity receive a higher number of stars.

Usability – How easy is it to use the application? Is there an intuitiveness to the controls or would a significant amount of instruction be necessary to help the user navigate the experience?

Content

There are many VR applications touted as "educational", but the amount of the content is very shallow or non-existent. The students rate the app based on its educational value.

Audio

We have found that some audio is necessary for narrating or enhancing the experience, while other experiences have audio that is distracting or difficult to discern.

Stability

We are running the software on above average gaming laptops that are connected to a school wireless network. Does the application run smoothly at all times or is it prone to crashing?

Overall

We take the average rating of the six categories to assign an overall rating.

Our final report shows the ratings of each individual category as well the overall. The breakdown allows educators to determine what fits their needs best. For example, if the primary concern of an educator is selecting an app with quality content and less worried about interactivity, they can choose accordingly.

The Research – What Do We Look For?

Students give their approval/disapproval tens or hundreds of times every day in digital applications. A single click allows students to like or love a post, picture, or meme. More often than not, this approval has to do with a picture of friends, a saying, or a meal. This is a quick assessment that usually does not involve much depth of thought, but rather a repetitive action.

My class is structured in a way where students are always working in pairs. We have 15 Oculus Rifts at our fingertips, which allows for maximum exposure to content in a reasonable amount of time. Students take turns inside the headset. While one student is navigating the experience, they are relaying information to their partner, who is taking notes in a shared Google Doc.

Students create a document containing every fact and impression gleaned from the activity. They make note of the positives and negatives they encounter. We do this so at the completion of the activity, students have documented evidence on which to base their final reviews.

In addition to forming their own informed opinions about each app, they also read as many reviews as they are able to find online. They are to systematically weigh each review for accuracy and look for bias. For instance, one VR app takes the user on a face-to-face interview with President Obama and the former first lady from within the White House. My students found negative reviews and 1-star ratings given by other users. But when taking a closer look, we found these reviews were written by people who had political stances against the former President and had nothing to do with the VR experience itself. Similarly, some negative reviews are given because the experience is educational and the user wanted a game, thus giving it a negative review. My students learn to categorize these reviews as irrelevant. They learn the value of testing the credibility of each review and not accepting the rating as gospel because there may be extenuating circumstances that led to the negative feedback.

Once both students have fully explored the educational VR app, looking under every rock and behind every tree, it is time to voice their opinion. They access a Google Form where they each enter their opinions, research, and ratings. The results are then compiled in a Google Sheet where I am able to average ratings and convert them into the familiar 5-star format.

Questions students answer in the VR app survey:

- What is the name of the application?
- Rate the application in the following areas
    - Motion/Nausea
    - Interactivity
    - Usability
    - Content
    - Audio
    - Stability
- What subject area does it address?
- What subject curriculum does the content fit within?

- What strand and standards does it cover?

- What do the online reviews say about the app?

- Are the reviews you read relevant to our purpose? Give an explanation.

- What are all the topics, terms, and concepts covered by the application?

- What positives did you find when using the app?

- What negatives did you find when using the app?

- What is your overall rating of the VR experience?

*Sample screenshots of the Google Form they fill out can be found in the appendix.

Two Examples of Our Ratings

The Anne Frank House VR

This experience is divided into two sections. The first is a narrated, guided tour of a VR version of the Anne Frank House. The user is taken through historical aspects of that period of her life. It incorporates quotes from her diary. The second part provides the user some increased interactivity and allows them to explore the house on their own. The narrator is still present to read quotes from her diary as they are displayed on the screen.

Overall	3.8	★ ★ ★ ☆ ☆
Motion	2.7	★ ★ ☆ ☆ ☆
Interactivity	4.3	★ ★ ★ ★ ☆
Useability	3.1	★ ★ ★ ☆ ☆
Content	4.5	★ ★ ★ ★ ☆
Audio	3.9	★ ★ ★ ☆ ☆
Stability	4.6	★ ★ ★ ★ ☆

Wonderful You

Wonderful You is an experience in VR with a small amount of interaction. The user is taken on a journey through the various sensory development stages of a fetus. Each of the 5 senses is explored individually with the help of stimulating graphics and visual effects.

Overall	4.2	★ ★ ★ ★ ☆
Motion	4.2	★ ★ ★ ★ ☆
Interactivity	4.3	★ ★ ★ ★ ☆
Useability	3.0	★ ★ ★ ☆ ☆
Content	4.6	★ ★ ★ ★ ☆
Audio	4.7	★ ★ ★ ★ ☆
Stability	4.3	★ ★ ★ ★ ☆

Benefits to Students

Students gain a number of benefits from taking the course. Besides learning to impartially evaluate a product, or application in this instance, they are required to effectively communicate in a variety of formats and they are exposed to educational content that touches many different subjects.

The evaluation exercise we do with VR apps requires thoughtful assessment of a product after in-depth testing. Before giving any app a review, students have the task of comprehensively researching and testing the product. During this process, they are required to inspect it looking through the lens of an educator and limit the innate tendency to look strictly for entertainment. This process incorporates justifying, defending, rating, supporting, categorizing, and outlining; all key aspects found in the framework of Bloom's Taxonomy. It requires the student to use critical thinking to gather information, synthesize it, and draw multiple conclusions. As students use higher order thinking skills, they are becoming independent thinkers.

These are important life skills in a world where instant gratification is so prevalent. With the swipe of a finger, you can be guaranteed 2-day delivery from Amazon or countless other retailers. We no longer wait in lines for take-out, instead we order ahead so we can bypass waiting in lines. And for a price, every amusement park offers some version of "Fast Pass". We have gotten away from enacting "wait time" before making purchases. Instead, we make impulsive decisions based on the first recommendation we read. After all, "if it's on the Internet it must be true, right?"

Another critical benefit gained from this process is improved communication and collaboration skills. Effective communication and collaboration are a soft skills that nearly every industry wants each employee to possess (Fiore et al., 2017). This class improves students' communication through relational interaction, written form, and group discussion. Doing the testing and research requires the student in the headset to effectively describe the content they are experiencing to the outside observer. This allows them to take detailed notes with accuracy. The written evaluation must be detailed to provide a comprehensive description the material. We try to avoid ambiguous explanations and improve clarity. Students learn to be specific in their assessments. Lastly, we hold regular group discussions on the pros and cons of a specific application. Students voice their concerns and offer up points and counterpoints. The group listens and considers all aspects before holding a class vote on whether the application is worthy of moving onto the next stage or bypassing it and moving on to the next one.

Finally, a pleasant byproduct of all this work is content exposure. While not the purpose of the class, it is a welcome result. Students are exposed to a variety of content, some of which is review from previous classes and some that is brand new. In both circumstances, students are either learning or reviewing vocabulary and concepts. This expands understanding and foundational knowledge.

Next Steps

The ultimate purpose of the class is to create lessons that incorporate VR and then assist a classroom teacher with the technology implementation.

After much research, evaluation, and discussion, the class generates a mini-lesson focused around a selected VR experience. A sample lesson designed by the students centered on "The

Raven VR" can be found in the appendix. Once complete, it includes the following:

- Synopsis of the activity

- Learning standards covered

- Materials needed

- Lesson timeline

- Pre and/or post activities

- Student handouts

- Teacher fact sheet (gives all information covered by the VR app)

Future advances in technology and in resources may increase the range and availability of VR application. Technology will be less cumbersome and distracting from the experience. Interest in VR among educational publishers will prompt additional materials in VR. However, we believe this model of engaging students in evaluating and delivery of VR could be useful in many ways, and can facilitate the adoption of VR technologies in schools. I have described this process from an educator's perspective; my students will share their own perspectives in the final chapter of the book.

References

Alia, Valerie (1997). "The Rashomon Principle: The Journalist as Ethnographer". In Alia, Valerie; Brennan, Brian; and Hoffmaster, Barry (eds.). *Deadlines and Diversity: Journalism Ethics in a Changing World*. Halifax, CAN: Fernwood.

Fiore, S. M., Graesser, A., Greiff, S., Griffin, P., Gong, B., Kyllonen, P., ... von Davier, A. (2017). *Collaborative Problem Solving: Considerations for the National Assessment of Educational Progress.* Alexandria VA: National Center for Education Statistics

7

VIEWING VIRTUAL REALITY FROM THE STUDENTS' PERSPECTIVE

_____

David Kaser and his students

We have spent a considerable amount of space examining the different aspects of using virtual reality in education. In this chapter we will spend some time hearing from some students who have been immersed in VR. At the time these articles were written, these four students were high school students in David Kaser's STEM VR class. In their own words, they will share their journeys into the world of VR, from the first time they put on a headset to where they foresee VR making an impact in education. One of the things I have learned in this journey using VR in a classroom is while adults have one idea of what "cool" and "innovative" consists of, student opinions may vary. Zach, Katie, Tyler, and Cara bring differing technology backgrounds to the table, but the one common thread they share is before enrolling in the STEM VR course is that they had little exposure to interactive 3D VR.

Zach, age 16, Junior

Virtual Reality (VR) has been a topic that has had periods of popularity throughout the years, seeing an extensive history of thought and development. Early attempts in the 1960s came through the efforts of Morton Hellig and his mechanical attempts in the Sensorama. However, major breakthroughs leading to today's use were pioneered by Ivan Sutherland who developed the impressive sounding 'Sword of Damocles,' widely considered to be the world's first head mounted device. Further developments came through academic and governmental research. Later, there were professional developments as virtual reality spread into a few industries including aerospace and entertainment. VR now, in the hands of technology companies along with recent advancements in micro computing, graphics, and software, is in the best place it has ever been. It was also at this point that I got to be involved through the efforts of the Science, Technology, Engineering, Mathematics (STEM): VR class and work with this amazing technology firsthand. From everything I've learned, my experiences, with VR parallel what I believe its general path will be in the near future. The hype that surrounds VR can give it unwarranted praise and applications. However, the fields where this technology can be applied will see a radical change due to its implementation.

I hadn't actively pursued the STEM: VR class, in fact, I hadn't even heard of it. I had heard of VR, but it was mostly through a gaming lens. Therefore, when I saw the class on my schedule, I was rather excited to research programs and evaluate their readiness for classroom integration. The first couple of weeks had been interesting, as none of the actual equipment we needed to get started had actually arrived yet. Therefore, with anticipation building, I mostly did some basic research on what VR actually was and how it was being used. I learned about things like haptic feedback, the physical response to a virtual interaction, and judder, the interruption of the image the user sees. I also started to learn about how VR was being used as it always had, with simulations for flight and the like. Then, one day, I came into the room and my instructor, Mr. Kaser, had on the head mounted display for the Oculus we had been waiting for weeks. I nearly jumped for joy.

Then I got to try it on.

Now, I could say many things about my first time in VR. I could describe how real the scenery felt, how I felt like I was right there. I could say that the low latency helped me seamlessly slide into the experience, that the sound stereo mixing made me hear things in a way I did not know you could with electronics. However, that will not really mean anything. People talked about that when I first watched them use VR, and it did not mean anything to me. It is something that is hard to describe, like the smell of a flower or the feeling of pain. It is something you need to experience to truly understand. I was amazed, and in truth, still am to some extent.

However, as with many new technologies, that is where the real problem with VR lies. The first couple of times you use it, you feel like this is the real future. That sparkle in your eyes makes you think anything can be improved with VR. Anything. That is how I first went into it, thinking that we could use it universally. However, that is just simply not the case. VR can be applied to many things, yes, but it is still a limited tool. My best example of this is from a program we tested early on by the name of "Big screen". At the time, it was a way for a VR user to have a 'virtual desktop', set in a constructed living room. And, unfortunately, it just did not work. The screen was too far away in the virtual environment, text just was not clear enough, and a whole other host of issues. To be granted, some issues were made by current technological limitations, however, others were caused by concept alone. Why would you want to use VR, this amazing tool, just to replicate your desktop with less precision and more latency?

That is not to say, however, that VR does not have strengths. At its current point, VR is amazing for conceptualization, interactivity, and breadth of scale. The project I worked most in depth on shows this well. We began working with the Anatomy & Physiology class at the high school, integrating sessions with VR into the class' structure. This was achieved using a program called Organon, basically a VR Anatomy textbook. Though I encountered a few stumbling blocks initially, such as controller interface, it was an incredible program. It allows for the 3D and accurate viewing of most any part of the endoskeleton system, in addition to common movements that show what all is active when you, for example, raise your arm. These movements can even be stopped, viewed, and rewinded. In addition, even though the sessions were mostly a contextual scavenger hunt, I found myself quite pleased with the results. Most students were actively engaged with the software, even after the 'wow factor' wore off. These students, partially through my actions, were more involved with and gained better understanding of the material.

There is many ideas as to why VR works well as an educational tool. The best software uses interactive to actively make the user engage with and use the program, getting it to better seat in the mind. Other software, even if merely a VR video, uses and envelopes the user more fully and allows them to use more of their brain to take in the information. Its integration of widely thought learning methods: spatial, visual, and auditory, make it a more inclusive and efficient form of teaching. Honestly, I am not sure about the science of it all. However, seeing more engaged students is something that sits well with me and it does just that.

The best part is that VR has not stopped growing. This year, VR company Oculus announced the release of their new "Oculus Odyssey", HTC released their wireless technology for HTC Vive systems, and more companies continue to jump into the ever widening fold of those that produce VR. As display and computing technology grows, VR will grow closer to reality in its ability to encapsulate the user. Growth has and will continue to occur in the development community, allowing better support for the increasing amount of people who are trying to develop software for it. These jumps in technology will lower the entry wall to VR and increase ease of use, making its implementation more effective.

When I first entered the STEM: VR course, I thought that I was going to be dealing with magic. Having gone through the experience, I now realize that view was somewhat naive. Some programs were just a waste of time, others still in long development cycles. The equipment itself, at times, was finicky to work with. Most importantly, not everything is enhanced by its integration. However, the gains I saw ignited in me a sort of magic: passion. Every time I saw a student put on a headset to get in the software and learn, confidence in the future of VR filled me. VR is a tool that has the ability to greatly impact education where it is used, for the better. At minimum, my interactions with VR made that year one of the most impactful of my education.

Katie, Age 17, Senior

What is VR? Well, if you are anything like me, you had no concept of what it was until this year. I even had to look up what it stood for: virtual reality. I entered blindly into the world of VR, with only two things on my mind: the hope that I would not mess up the expensive equipment, and the hope that I wouldn't fall over; both thoughts being influenced from stories I had heard about other's previous endeavors. VR was not an interest, not at first. It was not until I was placed in the virtual reality class at my high school that focused on reviewing apps and creating lesson plans around them, did I discover my fascination for the innovative technology. Through my personal experience with VR that left me awestruck, its educational potential became apparent to me.

After a few days of being thoroughly instructed on how to properly treat the equipment, which I relied heavily on my partner to help me with, it was time to disconnect from my world and immerse myself into the reality within the lens of the daunting black head set. Putting on the headset and adjusting what I needed to, a seemingly simple task was over complicated that day because of my nerves. My body was shaking involuntarily and my mind was racing, thinking about if I had the headset on correctly and what I was about to experience. Luckily, I had chosen a patient partner and before I was even mentally prepared, I was launched into the virtual world of the app.

The first app I used was called First Contact. It is a remedial app, designed to get the user well acquainted with the controls and how to navigate and interact with the imitation world they were in. I was in shock, but to my partner's dismay, not exactly speechless. Quite the opposite in fact. I could not grasp what I was experiencing and literal "oohs" and "ahhs" left my mouth as I stood in bewilderment. The app places a person in a spaceship ship setting and you are greeted with a helpful little robot, who seems to have been heavily influenced aesthetically by Wall-E. The friendly android instructs you to pick up things and play with different objects all in order to teach you what the triggers on the controls do. Before I was ready to be done, I had completed all the activities. I called for my partner to grab the controllers from my hands, and I carefully removed the headset.

"You do realize you said please and thank you, not only to a robot, but a completely virtual robot," my partner remarked.

I laughed it off, explaining I was preparing for the inevitable artificial intelligence takeover, but he was right. I had not realized at the time, but I made sure to be polite to the nonexistent robot because in the moment it felt so real. There was no distinguishing reality from virtual reality, the experience had been so immersive, I had used my manners out of habit.

Often times, the more one does something, the quicker the exciting novelty of the experience tends to wear off. Virtual reality seems to be one of the few exceptions. I attend VR class three times each week. I have been in the VR class for nine weeks now, and the amazement that accompanies using technology like this has yet to dwindle. I attribute this to the fact that each app offers a vastly different experience. For example, First Contact is very different from Anne Frank House or Titans of Space and many of the other apps we use. Not just through content, but the settings one is placed in, and the level of interactiveness each allows. Titans of Space in particular, is an app that is consistently fascinating. While the user experience is straightforward, one is placed on a spaceship touring the planets; the way in which it is carried out is incredible. During this experience, my partner suggested that I look over the side of my spaceship. When I did so, I had to catch my breath. Below me was space in it all its glory or what I could best conceive being in space was truly like. I began to get nervous that I might step off my platform and plummet into the deep dark matter around me and land amongst the glittering stars, when I reminded myself it was fake. At that moment, I had to look through the gap between the headset and my nose to see the very real, carpeted, classroom floor and stabilize my soaring thoughts and myself. In that moment, I was once again reminded of how startling virtual reality could be, and how lucky I was to be able to explore it.

While the VR experience is popular in the entertainment world, it also provides advantages and opportunities in an educational setting. Our class is tasked with testing apps and developing lesson plans around them, making the educational value apparent to me. I can already imagine the tentativeness surrounding using VR in an educational setting because of its association with video games; however choosing to purely focus on that miniscule aspect allows people to disregard the educational benefits of VR lessons. Virtual reality allows for a fully immersive experience that applies to multiple senses, which cannot be done in a traditional classroom Classrooms are filled different types of learners including visual, auditory, kinesthetic learners who rely on a combination of styles to absorb and retain as much information possible. Virtual reality appears to be one of the few technologies that meets the needs of various learners. Visually, the settings are stunning, whether it be because of the detail, art style, or presentation. Audibly, many apps include music, which makes the immersion even more convincing. Other apps read facts, quotes, and other information to students as they explore while it could be argued that students can reap the same benefits by looking at photos are watching videos, the kinesthetic aspect of learning I believe would be hard to recreate through traditional lesson plans and styles. Virtual reality gives learners the opportunity for hands-on learning, especially in classes other than science. VR allows students to ancient Egyptian tombs, the Anne Frank House, or the footsteps of a black sanitation worker during the Civil Rights Movement.

Beyond catering to different type of learners, lessons designed to incorporate virtual reality could motivate students. Education, although a luxury, is often seen by the student as a chore. VR could change that, getting students excited and engaged in their education. Learning should be about more than spewing out information in hopes a child retains it for their next test, state tests, ACT or SAT. As a senior in high school, I think about how enthusiastic I was about learning in early elementary school when things felt more like a game and there was more to succeeding than test scores. As I grew older, learning became tedious, and while I knew I enjoyed gaining new information, I no longer enjoyed school and its version of learning. I believe virtual reality has the ability to bring back that childlike wonder that accompanied learning. The technology has presented itself to society, and fits perfectly into an educational mold, failing to take advantage of this advancement in learning would be failing to better educate future generations of students. I can attest to its educational value from my personal experience and am intrigued by the positive effects it could have on the world of education.

Tyler, Age 17, Senior

Of all of the breakthroughs of technology in the last fifty years, the idea of entering a virtual world through VR is astonishing.

When I first put on the VR headset, the one thing that I had in mind was that I would still feel like I am holding the controllers and, to my surprise, which was not the case. Made specifically for the Oculus Rift, there are two controllers, made symmetrical to one another. Both have a specific shape to fit the hand very well, giving two triggers (one for the index finger, and the other for the middle finger). They have three buttons on top, two of which control the program and one that opens the oculus or program menus, and a joystick for either hand. Given those aspects of the controllers, they are very comfortable in one's hand, and the way that the headset fits as well allows me to forget about time entirely. When I loaded into First Contact VR, an application made for beginners starting up Oculus for the first time, I saw a robot that reminded me a lot of Wall-E, so I called him that. The situation seemed so surreal because I felt as though I was actually a part of it. In the experience, Wall-E was very shy to start, so he waves from behind a corner waiting for the player to wave back to him. He hands the player different objects that can do different things depending on what they do with that, so the player can appreciate every small detail; my favorite being the butterfly that lands on my finger when I kept it very still. Overall, the virtual experience was very enjoyable.

If this could be put into an educational setting, virtual reality can help students experience the topics they are covering in a completely new way. Hands-on learning is a key component to student's success, and VR provides that opportunity. For example, the program Organon VR, which would be used in Anatomy and Physiology, shows specific organs, bones, and different specific muscles allowing the students to see where they are or how they may be used with given descriptions. This provides students with a hands-on opportunity to learn while in the classroom. Without this opportunity, students would be relying primarily on traditional methods such as textbooks and notes.

VR attracts a majority of users' attention because it is very unheard of, and not too many people have been able to afford a good computer and a VR headset such as the Oculus Rift. Funding in education is a challenge as is, and the cost of adding VR to a school budget presents another layer. At Barberton High School, the way that this problem was solved was that the STEM teacher wrote a grant for the money needed to buy the fifteen Oculus Rifts as well as the fifteen computers needed to run said Oculus Rifts. Students were included in the grant writing process, as we were responsible for researching the advantages to including VR in the education setting.

Cara, Age 16, Junior

At first glance, Virtual Reality (VR) looked like a fun gaming experience because of all of the articles I read about people who talked about the great time they had inside of the headsets. Many people have watched videos of people playing Beat Saber, and wished they had their own headset to play around with. My first encounter with VR was actually at Cedar Point on the Iron Dragon Coaster. Using a Samsung Gear VR headset, the engineers took the story with the motion of the ride to make the rider feel like they are on a completely different ride. The only downfall was that it was a complete ghost story, without interaction. Through my personal experiences, I have realized that VR has enormous potential for education and in the future.

I had never experienced VR in an educational setting, and thought it was only used by gamers and YouTubers. I then registered for Science Technology Engineering Mathematics (STEM) VR class in high school, and used an interactive headset for the first time. In class, we used an Oculus Rift and played First Contact VR, which helped us understand how the Rift Controllers work. The game shows players that the controllers can sense how their hands move and what they are doing at the same time. This first time created a euphoric moment for me.

While VR is popular in the gaming world, it provides new opportunities to students today. Students benefit from hands-on, active learning now more than ever, which makes VR an ideal teaching tool. For example, VR can be used to learn about world history. In our STEM VR class, we went on a virtual tour through the Anne Frank House. The app shows Anne Frank's life and what she had to do to hide from the Nazis. Anne Frank is included in most high school curriculum, but it is usually taught in a traditional classroom setting with visual aids such as photos. In some cases, teachers may also use video clips. VR technology enhances student learning because they actually feel like they are in the house. It creates a more meaningful experience for students, which has a great impact on their learning.

After the virtual tour of Anne Frank's house, we helped create a lesson plan to teach other students about the house. We picked activities to go along with the VR experience to help students understand the topic better. We have not executed the lesson plan yet with a class, but have done the in-depth research and planning. This helped show me that my understanding of the topic has increased even more because I have gone over the topic of Anne Frank multiple times. I want to see how more classrooms create lesson plans in the future.

I think VR will be a regular use in the classroom in the future. The headsets have an infinite number of classes they could be used for. It will change how teachers present materials to students. Anatomy students will be able to learn about the body without breaking out books and plastic skeletons. The future of VR in classrooms is looking better than ever and the possibilities are endless.

8

CONCLUSION

A few themes emerge across this collection of articles when considering new technology in the classroom. First and foremost, technology use should be guided by learning goals, as they are central to the selection of technology and content to be delivered. The challenge of limited funding resources is an opportunity to find local resources in empowering students in helping select equipment, curate and even create content, and support technology going forward. Building a community includes finding colleagues who can be supportive and finding ways to bring the technology to the audience early on to garner additional support. Students can be helpful in partnering with teachers to implement VR technology in their classrooms. Innovations in technology are always evolving, and a clear vision for how the new approaches can be integrated is essential. Students can also help by monitoring the current models and suggesting new directions for keeping virtual reality – or the next innovation – moving forward in your school.

So where does that leave us? Virtual reality will not, in itself, revolutionize education, however, we believe it can provide a valuable new dimension for exploring content and concepts. We have evidence that students agree, as they describe how their enthusiasm for the new technology is sustained as a learning experience even after the initial novelty. Virtual reality has the potential to be a powerful tool in learning, with the right support and content. Additionally, we believe the examples and teaching practices contained in these pages have ideas about feasibility and sustainability that carry lasting relevance in the face of ever-changing technology. We encourage you to share your own stories and tips with us and with a wider community at our website, envisionXR.net. We hope these ideas and stories help you in envisioning virtual reality.

Part III

About the
Authors

9

MEREDITH THOMPSON ED.D.

BIO

Early on, I remember being fascinated by science. My mom and my dad encouraged and supported this interest. One of my goals is to share my passion with other people.

I am currently a research scientist and lecturer for the Scheller Teacher Education Program. I'm interested in learning how people work collaboratively, how to use games to help students learn, and how to use virtual and simulated environments for learning STEM topics. I studied chemistry at Cornell, have a master's in science and engineering education from Tufts, and a doctorate in science education from Boston University. I have two current projects: the Collaborative Learning Environments for Virtual Reality (CLEVR) is creating a cross platform collaborative game about cellular biology, and INSPIRE is a group of education professors who are using games and simulations in teacher preparation. I also use games and simulations when I teach the

STEP course: "Understanding and Evaluating Education." I think VR can be a powerful tool in learning, however, technology does not revolutionize education – educators, engaging learning activities, and well planned implementations are essential to success.

In my spare time, I write and sing music with my twin sister Chris (www.cmthompson.com), write poetry, and enjoy hiking in the woods with my two sons and my dog.

10

DAVID KASER

───────────

STEM Teacher - Barberton High School

BIO

───────────

When I think of VR and the role it can play in education, I see possibilities. The possibility that allows abstract material to suddenly make sense for the student who is a concrete thinker. The possibility to show the spatial relationships a 2-dimensional drawing struggles to justify. The possibility that allows the creative mind to produce spatial art in a medium that is relatively new and untapped. Yet at the same time, it is just another tool. Without effective planning and instruction, it is a gimmick. The power of VR lies in the hands of two groups of people: programmers who design quality content and effective teachers who realize the key to effective instruction does not lie in the tools, but in lesson design and relationships.

I am a 20-year teaching veteran, having spent my entire career in the Barberton City School District, a 2019 Ohio finalist for the

PAEMST award, and a finalist for the 2019 State of Ohio Teacher of the Year. I graduated from the University of Akron for both my undergraduate and master's degrees. I began my career teaching middle school mathematics and science. Over the years, my work with technology integration opened the door to teach computer applications. During this time, I began serving as a building technology coordinator, a position I still currently hold. I have had the privilege to design, create, and implement both the middle school and high school's STEM programs in Barberton. I was honored to be selected as the ITIP State of Ohio Outstanding Technology-Using Teacher Award in 2018, recognized by ISTE as a Make It Happen educator, granted the Martha Holden Jennings' Arthur S. Holden Teacher Award for Excellence in Science Education in 2012, and was selected to the Summit County All-Star Teaching Team in 2014. Recently my work implementing virtual reality in education has opened doors to collaborate with fellow educators and is featured on the Google for Education Transformation Center webpage.

II

KARA GRIJALVA

———

BIO

———

I am an international development practitioner specializing in evidence-driven education programs in low-resource and conflict-affected communities, including managing ICT programs across Africa and Asia. I have an M.Ed in International Education Policy from the Harvard Graduate School of Education and M.A in Development Management from SIT Graduate Institute.

Part IV

Appendix

12

THE RAVEN VR SAMPLE LESSON

David Kaser and his students

MEREDITH THOMPSON, DAVID KASER, AND KARA GRIJVALA

THE RAVEN VR

SYNOPSIS

Students will experience a VR experience based on The Raven. They will work on vocabulary acquisition in multiple ways. Students will apply their understanding and new vocabulary in an activity using Twitter as a basis for sharing ideas.

The Raven VR is an audio and visual experience based on the literary masterpiece "The Raven" by Edgar Allen Poe. The app offers a narrated reading of the poem while placing the user in a room with visual representations. The VR experience itself lasts 10 minutes.

TIMELINE

This activity is designed to take be completed in 3 - 45 minute sessions.

MATERIALS

- Oculus Rift
- Oculus controller/Touch
- The Raven Activity sheets
- Notecards printed with the Twitter graphic.
- Timeline hung across one side of the room to hang the "live" tweets.

ACTIVITY DESCRIPTION

Divide the students into pairs. The pairs will work together on all three parts of the mini-lesson.

Pre-VR Activity: Reading, visualization, unfamiliar word identification

VR Activity: Partners go through the audio/visual VR experience, relaying descriptions about the visual representation of The Raven and contextual clues that helps with defining unfamiliar words.

Post-VR Activity: Live Twitter updates

CREATED BY THE BARBERTON HIGH SCHOOL VR TEAM

TIMELINE

Day 1
- Divide students into pairs. It is possible to work as an individual, but groups of 3 become more difficult to manage.
- Hand out student Pre-VR activity sheets and a copy of the Raven.
- Students will read the poem with their partner and complete the student activity sheet.
- If time allows, hold a class discussion on how they visualize aspects of the poem.

Days 2
- VR students will setup the VR equipment and be available to help content classes use it.
- Student pairs will take turns experiencing the Raven VR.
- Students will communicate with their partner items of importance from the VR experience while their partner documents it on the student activity sheet.
- If needed, the students should be able to go through the VR experience a second time.

Day 3
- Students will work with their partner on creating a minimum of 3 "live" tweets on the supplied notecards. They should take the point of view of the main character.
    - Students must use at least one "unfamiliar" word in each of their "live" tweets.
- Optional, create poem timeline and have students post their "live" tweets along the timeline.
- Students should also read other groups "live" tweets.
- Hold a class discussion on the poem, meaning, visualization of their preconceived ideas and the VR experience, "live" tweets, etc.

CREATED BY THE BARBERTON HIGH SCHOOL VR TEAM

STANDARDS

English 9:

RL.9-10.4 Determine the meaning of words and phrases as they are used in the text, including figurative and connotative meanings; analyze the cumulative impact of specific word choices on meaning, mood, and tone (e.g., how the language evokes a sense of time and place or an emotion; how it sets a formal or informal tone).

RL.9-10.10 By the end of grade 10, read and comprehend literature, including stories, dramas, and poems, at the high end of the grades 9–10 text complexity band independently and proficiently, building background knowledge and activating prior knowledge in order to make personal, historical, and cultural connections that deepen understanding of complex text.

RL. 9 – 10.7 Analyze the representation of a subject or a key scene in two different types of artistic mediums, including what is emphasized or absent in each.

RL. 9-10.1 Cite strong and thorough textual evidence to support analysis of what the text says explicitly as well as inferences drawn from the text.

CREATED BY THE BARBERTON HIGH SCHOOL VR TEAM

ACTIVITY

READING AND IMAGINATION

1. Read "The Raven" together. Visualize the poem.

2. Write down unfamiliar words you and your partner encounter.

3. Use context clues from the poem. What do you think these words mean?

4. What does the setting look like (write it down or draw it on the back of this page)?

5. What does the main character look like (write it down or draw)?

6. What are some other parts of the poem you can visualize? What does it look like?

CREATED BY THE BARBERTON HIGH SCHOOL VR TEAM

VR ACTIVITY

The Raven VR Experience: As you go through the VR experience, tell your partner things you notice about the visual representation of the poem or contextual clues that help you understand any of your unfamiliar words from the pre-VR activity.

Live Tweeting: Time to put on the shoes of the main character. You and your partner are to create 3 "live" tweets. Keep in mind Twitter has character limits. You must use at least 1 unfamiliar word correctly in each tweet. Be creative.

CREATED BY THE BARBERTON HIGH SCHOOL VR TEAM

Edgar Allan Poe ✓
@LenoreisDead

Following ⌄

7:36 PM - 29 Jan 1849

7,741 Retweets **25,814** Likes

💬 13K ⟲ 7.7K ♡ 26K ✉

13

VR APP EVALUATION

David Kaser

Below are three screenshots of the survey students use when researching, testing, and evaluating a VR experience. It is not the entire form, but it paints a picture of the type of feedback they are required to give when they are done. I use their feedback to create the 5-star ratings described in the "Student Voice Counts" chapter.

VR Software Evaluation

Use this form to evaluate the software you have researched, downloaded, and tested.

* Required

Group Members *
First and last name

Your answer

Computer Number *

Choose ▼

What is the name of the app/experience/software? *

Your answer

Motion - Comfort level *

	1	2	3	4	5	
Causes motion sickness	○	○	○	○	○	Very comfortable

Content *

	1	2	3	4	5	
Very little educational value	○	○	○	○	○	Quality educational content

Interactiveness *

	1	2	3	4	5	
100% Ghost Story	○	○	○	○	○	Allows user to navigate and choose experiences

Useability - intuitiveness of UI (user interface) - Ease of use *

	1	2	3	4	5	
Difficult to figure out controls and navigate	○	○	○	○	○	Very easy to use

Stability *

	1	2	3	4	5	
App crashes frequently	○	○	○	○	○	App never crashes

Audio *

	1	2	3	4	5	
Distracting audio/talking is difficult to understand	○	○	○	○	○	Effective use of sound/talking/information presentation

Purchasing platform *

☐ Oculus store

☐ Steam

What Strand AND Standard does it cover? (may be multiple)
Example: 1. Earth Systems - The Planets and Their Moons -
Identify and describe the properties of the of the inner planets.
2. Earth Systems - The Historical and Theoretical Advances in
Astronomy - Research the types of spacecraft and missions
used to explore the universe *

Your answer

What is the cost? *

Your answer

Describe and summarize the reviews you found online *

Your answer

Are the reviews you read online relevant to our goals and
research? Explain. *

Your answer

Give a summary of what is covered by the software. *

Your answer

When you tested it, what positives did you find (user
interface/usability/glitches/how information is
presented/interactivity/etc)? *

Your answer

About the ETC Press

The ETC Presswas founded in 2005 under the direction of Dr. Drew Davidson, the Director of Carnegie Mellon University's Entertainment Technology Center (ETC), as an academic, digital-first (but not digital only), open access publishing imprint.

What does all that mean?

The ETC Press publishes academic and trade books and singles, textbooks, academic journals, and conference proceedings that focus on issues revolving around entertainment technologies as they are applied across a variety of fields. Our authors come from a range of fields. Some are traditional academics. Some are practitioners. And some work in between. What ties them all together is their ability to write about the impact of emerging technologies and its significance in society.

In keeping with that mission, the ETC Press uses emerging technologies to design all of our books and Lulu, an on-demand publisher, to distribute our e-books and print books through all the major retail chains, such as Amazon, Barnes & Noble, Kobo, and Apple, and we work with The Game Crafter to produce tabletop games.

We don't carry an inventory ourselves. Instead, each print book is created when somebody buys a copy.

The ETC Press is also an open-access publisher, which means every book, journal, and proceeding is available as a free download. We're most interested in the sharing and spreading of ideas. We also have an agreement with the Association for Computing Machinery (ACM) to list ETC Press publications in the ACM Digital Library.

Because we're an open-access publisher, authors retain ownership of their intellectual property. We do that by releasing all of our books, journals, and proceedings under one of two Creative Commons licenses:

- Attribution-NoDerivativeWorks-NonCommercial: This license allows for published works to remain intact, but versions can be created.

- Attribution-NonCommercial-ShareAlike: This license allows for authors to retain editorial control of their creations while also encouraging readers to collaboratively rewrite content.

This is definitely an experiment in the notion of publishing, and we invite people to participate. We are exploring what it means to "publish" across multiple media and multiple versions. We believe this is the future of publication, bridging virtual and physical media with fluid versions of publications as well as enabling the creative blurring of what constitutes reading and writing.